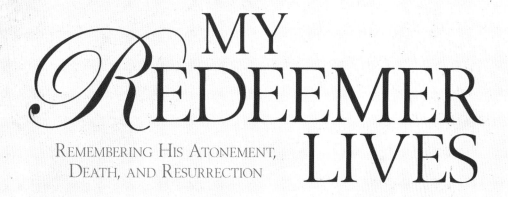

My Redeemer Lives

Remembering His Atonement, Death, and Resurrection

Cover image: *Divine Redeemer* © 2009 Simon Dewey. Courtesy of Altus Fine Art. www.altusfineart.com.

Published by Covenant Communications, Inc.
American Fork, Utah

Text by Kathryn B. Jenkins. Copyright © 2009 by Covenant Communications, Inc.
All rights reserved. No part of this book may be reproduced in any format or in any medium without the written permission of the publisher, Covenant Communications, Inc., P.O. Box 416, American Fork, UT 84003. This work is not an official publication of The Church of Jesus Christ of Latter-day Saints. The views expressed within this work are the sole responsibility of the author and do not necessarily reflect the position of The Church of Jesus Christ of Latter-day Saints, Covenant Communications, Inc., or any other entity.

Printed in China
First Printing: September 2009

15 14 13 12 10 09   10 9 8 7 6 5 4 3 2 1

ISBN-13: 978-1-59811-789-9
ISBN-10: 1-59811-789-0

MY REDEEMER LIVES

Remembering His Atonement, Death, and Resurrection

Introduction

It is a matter of history that, at or near the beginning of what has since come to be known as the Christian era, the Man Jesus, surnamed the Christ, was born in Bethlehem of Judea. The principal data as to His birth, life, and death are so well attested as to be reasonably indisputable; they are facts of record, and are accepted as essentially authentic by the civilized world at large. True, there are diversities of deduction based on alleged discrepancies in the records of the past as to circumstantial details; but such differences are of strictly minor importance, for none of them nor all taken together cast a shadow of reasonable doubt upon the historicity of the earthly existence of the Man known in literature as Jesus of Nazareth.

—James E. Talmage[1]

Mankind has never produced a leader to rank with Jesus of Nazareth.

"Once or twice in a thousand years—perhaps a dozen times since mortal man became of dust a living soul—an event of such transcendent import occurs that neither heaven nor earth are ever thereafter the same," proclaimed Elder Bruce R. McConkie. "Once or twice in a score of generations the hand from heaven clasps the hand on earth in perfect fellowship, the divine drama unfolds, and the whole course of mortal events changes."[2]

There can be no greater example of such fellowship than the birth, life, and death of Jesus Christ. Mankind has never produced a leader to rank with Jesus of Nazareth. Even if we regard Him only in historic perspective, says Talmage, He is unique. He stands supreme among men simply by reason of the excellence of His personal character, the genuine worth of His teachings, and the influence of His example.

"Christian and unbeliever alike acknowledge His supremacy as a Man, and respect the epoch-making significance of His birth," Talmage writes. "Christ was born in the meridian of time; and His life on earth marked at once the culmination of the past and the inauguration of an era distinctive in human hope, endeavor, and achievement."

Christ's birth, in fact, was such a pivotal event that the world reckons time in relation to it. Talmage further writes, "The rise and fall of dynasties, the birth and dissolution of nations, all the cycles of history as to war and peace, as to prosperity and adversity, as to health and pestilence, seasons of plenty and of famine, the awful happenings of earthquake and storm, the triumphs of invention and discovery, the epochs of man's development in godliness and the long periods of his dwindling in unbelief—all the occurrences that make history—are chronicled throughout Christendom by reference to the year before or after the birth of Christ."[3]

But for us, those distinguishing characteristics—characteristics that Talmage refers to as surpassing greatness—significant as they are, fail to distinguish what made this man the Savior of all mankind. To these distinguishing characteristics is added an attribute that far exceeds the sum of all the others: His origin is divine. We proclaim the eternal reality of His

*F*or according to the great plan of the Eternal God there must be an atonement made, or else all mankind must unavoidably perish. . . .

ALMA 34:9

status as Lord and God. And we testify boldly that He did for us what we could not possibly do for ourselves.

His wondrous yet natural birth and His immaculate life in the flesh deserve what Talmage calls "our reverent attention."[4] Yet those things are not what lift us up—what make of us, as mere humans, all that we could ever be and more than we could ever hope. The offer of salvation to even the most wretched soul among us comes as a result of His voluntary death as a consecrated sacrifice for the sins of mankind—what we know as the Atonement.

That Atonement—the gift that makes it possible for us to return as sanctified beings to the Father who created us all, to dwell forever in His presence—is what brings us to the waters of baptism. It is what brings us each week to the sacrament table in renewal of our covenant to always remember Him, to keep His commandments. It is what brings us to our knees in repentance. It is what makes of our sorrow the possibility of deep and quenching joy. It is what makes of us new creatures, qualified in every way for exaltation.

That gift freely given, that Atonement, actually began on a still night in a crude stall in Bethlehem, for at the moment of His birth, He began reconciling us with the Father. "The Immortal God was His Father, and the mortal Mary was His mother," Elder Bruce R. McConkie testified. "And it was in consequence of this birth—a birth in which mortality and immortality joined hands—that He was able to perform His atoning mission and put into operation the great and eternal plan of redemption."[5] Every act of His mortal life was one more step in restoring us to that Being who gave us life. The final acts of His life, those we will here examine, represent a series of events in which the greatest man who ever lived performed the greatest sacrifice ever made—without which our existence would have no meaning or purpose.

"In its sweep and scope, atonement takes on the aspect of one of the grand constants in nature—omnipresent, unalterable, such as gravity or the speed of light," observed Hugh Nibley. "Like them it is always there, easily ignored, hard to explain, and hard to believe in without an explanation. Also, we are constantly exposed to its effects whether we are aware of them or not. . . . Like gravity, though we are rarely aware of it, it is at work every moment of our lives, and to ignore it can be fatal. It is waiting at our disposal to draw us on."[6]

Behold, he sendeth an invitation unto all men, for the arms of mercy are extended towards them, and he saith: Repent, and I will receive you.

Alma 5:33

THE Last Supper

In superb allegory the Lord [illustrated] the vital relationship between the apostles and Himself, and between Himself and the Father, by the figure of a vinegrower, a vine, and its branches. . . . A grander analogy is not to be found in the world's literature. Those ordained servants of the Lord were as helpless and useless without Him as is a bough severed from the tree. . . . those men, though ordained to the Holy Apostleship, would find themselves strong and fruitful in good works, only as they remained in steadfast communion with the Lord. Without Christ what were they, but unschooled Galileans, some of them fishermen, one a publican, the rest of undistinguished attainments, and all of them weak mortals? As branches of the Vine they were at that hour clean and healthful, through the instructions and authoritative ordinances with which they had been blessed, and by the reverent obedience they had manifested.

—James E. Talmage[7]

As the poet tells us, "Our birth is but a sleep and a forgetting: The Soul that rises with us, our life's Star, Hath had elsewhere its setting, And cometh from afar . . . trailing clouds of glory do we come From God, who is our home" (William Wordsworth, "Ode: Intimations of Immortality"). For each of us comes the time, that singular moment on an eternal continuum, when physical death occurs and the spirit soars heavenward—to that God, who is our home.

We know, sure as the sun rises in the east, that such a moment will arrive. Yet we who are tethered by mortality go about our earthly routines not knowing at what instant our work will be finished. Circumstances must, of necessity, have been different for the Savior—He whose sandaled feet walked by the will of the Father—as He approached the tumultuous cascade of events that would culminate in His death and Resurrection. It occurs to us that He knew.

Knowing that His time on earth was drawing to a close—and without doubt dreading the painful ordeal that lay ahead of Him—it must have been with heavy heart and with utter tenderness that He prepared to partake of the paschal meal with those He most loved, the Twelve He had chosen to walk by His side. But this was no simple feast, no ordinary Host. This supper represented to all of Israel that the pure lamb had been sacrificed, and none could anticipate how quickly their symbolic celebration would become literal rather than figurative.

Jesus arrived with the Twelve at "a large upper room furnished" (Luke 22:12), and together they sat down to the last meal the Savior would partake of before His death. Under what Talmage calls the "strain of profound emotion," Jesus told those gathered around the feast, "I have desired to eat this passover with you before I suffer: For I say unto you, I will not any more eat thereof, until it be fulfilled in the kingdom of God" (Luke 22:15–16). Now the disciples, too, knew.

Now the feast of unleavened bread drew nigh, which is called the Passover. And when the hour was come, he sat down, and the twelve apostles with him.

LUKE 22:1, 14

The supper, says Talmage, went forward with tense sadness. As those in the upper room—borrowed, just as would be His tomb—solemnly ate, the Savior sorrowfully uttered, "One of you which eateth with me shall betray me" (Mark 14:18). Astonishment washed over the supplicants gathered around the table. All but one—allied at that moment with Perdition—gazed inwardly with bewilderment for even a kernel

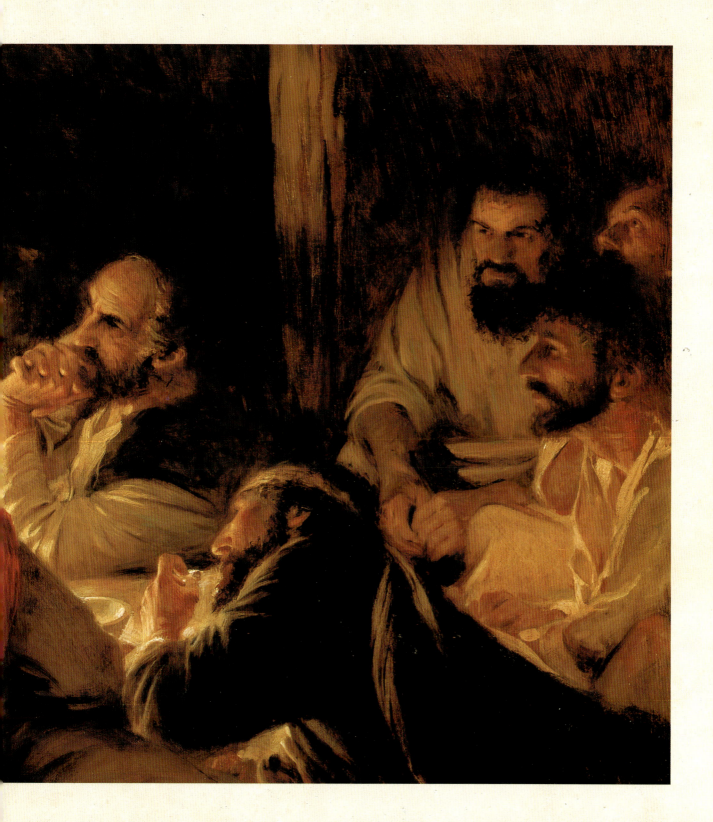

of doubt. One after another exclaimed with shock, "Is it I?" (Mark 14:19). Talmage gives us keen insight into the character of the disciples gathered there when he tells us that "each of those who so inquired was more concerned with the dread thought that possibly he was an offender, however inadvertently so, than as to whether his brother was about to prove himself a traitor."[8]

Perhaps we, with the Eleven, are caused to examine our own hearts for any trace of betrayal that might linger there. Any infidelity on our part could never compare in magnitude to what happened that night almost two thousand years ago. But are we, driven by our human natures, at risk of betraying Him as we regard too lightly His sacrifice for us and take too lightly His counsel?

We know that one—one who had already covenanted to sell his Master for thirty pieces of silver—asked with brazen audacity, "Master, is it I?" The Lord—who knows each heart—responded with cutting promptness: "Thou hast said" (Matt. 26:25). Of that Judas Iscariot, the Lord confirmed, "good were it for that man if he had never been born" (Mark 14:21). With his fingers clutched tightly around the purse concealed within his robes, that Judas would within the hour make his way out into the inky darkness to finish his treachery.

Two other singular events set this supper apart from all others. Rising from the table and laying aside his outer garments, Jesus fashioned about Himself a towel as an apron. Then, taking a basin filled with water, He knelt before each of the Twelve and tenderly washed and dried the feet of those who knew Him best and who loved Him most fiercely.

It is easy to imagine that these humble servants initially resisted what they saw as a menial act performed by He who was greatest among them all.

He said, "He that is greatest among you shall be your servant," and gave us the great example when washing his disciples' feet.

PRESIDENT N. ELDON TANNER, "LEADING AS THE SAVIOR LED," *NEW ERA*, JUNE 1977

To these unassuming men gathered around the paschal table had not yet come the understanding that what the Savior brought with a simple basin of water was so much more than the mere rinsing of dust and dirt from the weary feet of devoted disciples.

Apparently Peter was the first to give voice to their reluctance when he asked, "Lord, dost thou wash my feet?" (John 13:6). As the disciples had come to expect, the response of the Savior packed an eternity of meaning into a sparse handful of words— "What I do thou knowest not now"—while giving the fisherman hope for deeper eventual discernment: "but thou shalt know hereafter" (John 13:7).

Still Peter resisted. For three years he had followed this Prophet, had witnessed miracles, had seen lame men walk and dead men live again. We can only imagine that Peter's objection became more vehement as he declared with resolute firmness, "Thou shalt never wash my feet" (John 13:8).

Undeterred, the Savior brought clarity to the importance of the ordinance with a simple ultimatum: "If I wash thee not, thou hast no part with me" (John 13:8). Still not understanding, Peter—the weathered man of the seas

> *In this "simple but impressive manner was instituted the ordinance, since known as the Sacrament of the Lord's Supper."*
>
> JAMES E. TALMAGE, *JESUS THE CHRIST*

who had been crafted and polished by daily interaction with the greatest who ever lived—thrust forth both his hands and his feet and implored, "Lord, not my feet only, but also my hands and my head" (John 13:9). The sudden reality of being left behind was undoubtedly too terrible to contemplate.

In the simple bathing of feet—symbolic not only of the much greater sacrifice to come over the ebb and flow of the next few days, but of a lifetime lived only for others—Jesus taught a profound lesson for the Twelve and for all of us who yearn to be called His disciples: "Know ye what I have done to you? Ye call me Master and Lord: and ye say well; for so I am. If I then, your Lord and Master, have washed your feet; ye also ought to wash one another's feet. For I have given you an example, that ye should do as I have done to you" (John 13:12–15). Patiently, the greatest of them all taught not only the Twelve, but the least of us all, a pattern for living, a pattern for returning with Him to our Father.

Kneeling before them, the Lord gave His anxious disciples a glimpse of even more when He assured them that the washing made them "clean every whit" (John 13:10)—just as the incomparable Atonement, only hours away, would give all who ever lived the chance to emerge from mortality clean, every whit.

And then there came the crowning act of this supper: the Lord returned to the table, bowed His head, and blessed a loaf of unleavened bread. Breaking it and giving a portion to each of His disciples, He bid them, "This is my body which is given for you: this do in remembrance of me" (Luke 22:19). Once they had eaten, He blessed a cup of wine and passed it among His disciples, saying, "Drink ye all of it; For this is my blood of the new testament, which is shed for many for the remission of sins" (Matt. 26:27–28).

In this "simple but impressive manner was instituted the ordinance, since known as the Sacrament of the Lord's Supper," Talmage tells us. "The bread and wine, duly consecrated by prayer, become emblems of the Lord's body and blood, to be eaten and drunk reverently, and in remembrance of Him."[9]

Two millennia later, each of us has been told, "And that thou mayest more fully keep thyself unspotted from the world, thou shalt go to the house of prayer and offer up thy sacraments upon my holy day" (D&C 59:9).

For I have given you an example, that ye should do as I have done to you.

John 13:15

In our longing to be unspotted, we as His disciples still come to the sacrament table. There the bread lies broken—much like the Savior's body in the borrowed tomb, and much like our own hearts. There it is covered with white linen—again, much like the Savior's body in the borrowed tomb. The linen is white not only as a symbol of purity, but as a symbol of victory: a reminder to us that Christ is the victor over death and sin.

Preparing to leave the upper room and travel the lonely highway to Gethsemane, the Lord gave His disciples a new commandment: that they love one other as He had loved them (see John 13:34). He then told them, "By this shall all men know that ye are my disciples, if ye have love one to another" (John 13:35).

"The law of Moses enjoined mutual love among friends and neighbors; but the new commandment, by which the apostles were to be governed, embodied love of a higher order," Talmage explains. "They were to love one another as Christ loved them; and their brotherly affection was to be a distinguishing mark of their apostleship, by which the world would recognize them as men set apart."[10]

In that agonizing moment before He began His last walk up the gentle slope of the Mount of Olives, the Savior tenderly told His loved ones, "Whither I go, ye cannot come" (John 13:33). Peter—offering to lay down his life for His Master's sake—asserted his readiness to follow, even to death, rather than be separated from his Lord. Yet this chief Apostle, this "Man of Rock" as Talmage calls him, had yet to be fully changed and converted himself—for as the Lord predicted, "the cock shall not crow this day, before that thou shalt thrice deny that thou knowest me" (Luke 22:34).

In His tender dialogue with His disciples, the Lord had, according to Talmage,

> . . . affirmed His own inherent Godship, and through their trust in Him and obedience to His requirements would they find the way to follow whither He was about to precede them. Thomas, that loving, brave, though somewhat skeptical soul, desiring more definite information ventured to say: "Lord, we know not whither thou goest; and how can we know the way?" The Lord's answer was a reaffirmation of His divinity; "I am the way, the truth, and the life: no man cometh

The Son of God commenced His earthly ministry with an ordinance—baptism—and ended His ministry with an ordinance—the sacrament. Both bore record of His death, burial, and resurrection . . . .

David B. Haight, "Remembering the Savior's Atonement," Ensign, April 1988

unto the Father, but by me. If ye had known me, ye should have known my Father also: and from henceforth ye know him, and have seen him."[11]

His message to His disciples stands for us today: it is through Him, and through Him only, that we can come to know the Father. Not only is He our advocate with the Father, but His Atonement provides the only way by which we can be made clean, the only path by which we can approach the Father and stand unspotted and pure before Him.

It is difficult for us to grasp the power of emotion that must have filled that upper room late on the night of the paschal supper. Jesus of Nazareth stood on the threshold of the most incomprehensible and remarkable sacrifice ever made; He faced betrayal of the most base kind, utter loneliness in a situation of complete despair, pain more exquisite than could be borne by mortal man. Those who loved Him and now gathered about Him, imploring, faced losing Him—and, because they couldn't understand, thought they were losing Him forever. At that tender moment He reached out to them in His infinite love as He told them, "I will not leave you comfortless: I will come to you" (John 14:18).

To the disciples straining to cling to Him, Talmage tells us, Jesus "graciously explained that they would soon weep and lament while the world rejoiced; this had reference to His death; but He promised that their sorrow should be turned into joy; and this was based on His resurrection to which they should be witnesses. He compared their then present and prospective state to that of a woman in travail, who in the after joy of blessed motherhood forgets her anguish. The happiness that awaited them would be beyond the power of man to take away. . . ."[12]

Our most valuable worship experience in the sacrament meeting is the sacred ordinance of the sacrament, for it provides the opportunity to focus our minds and hearts upon the Savior and His sacrifice.

DAVID B. HAIGHT, "THE SACRAMENT—AND THE SACRIFICE," *ENSIGN*, APRIL 2007

Isn't that how it is for us? In our humanity, in our weakness and failings we stray from Him and break commandments. We lament, and we suffer the deep and anguished sorrow of one who regrets submitting to temptation. Because of the Atonement, because of the sacrifice borne not only of a love we can't even comprehend but of a desire to do the Father's will, our sorrow can be turned into joy. And the happiness that awaits us will be beyond the power of any man to take away.

And so concluded what we have come to know as the last supper. It drew to a close, says Talmage, with "a prayer such as could be addressed to none but the Eternal Father, and such as none but the Son of that Father could offer...."[13]

Concluding with a hymn, Jesus and the Eleven went out to the Mount of Olives.

What remnants of that supper remain with us today? Certainly a command to love deeply, in a way that identifies us forever as His disciples. Certainly the ability to partake of the sacrament, placing our broken hearts on the altar and receiving in return His magnificent Spirit to be with us. And certainly the beginning of that Atoning sacrifice that gives each of us the ability to be worthy—to inherit eternal life.

I have glorified thee on the earth: I have finished the work which thou gavest me to do.

John 17:4–5

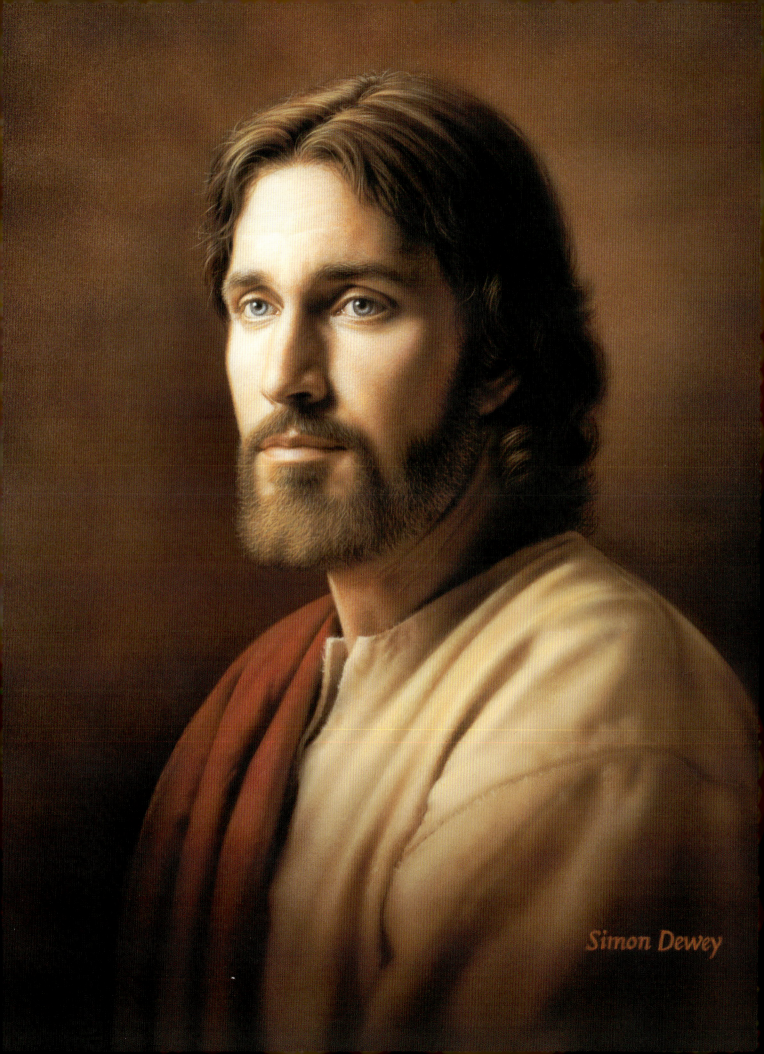

THE GARDEN OF GETHSEMANE

    Christ's agony in the garden is unfathomable by the finite mind, both as to intensity and cause. . . . He struggled and groaned under a burden such as no other being who has lived on earth might even conceive as possible. It was not physical pain, nor mental anguish alone, that caused Him to suffer such torture as to produce an extrusion of blood from every pore; but a spiritual agony of soul such as only God was capable of experiencing. . . . In that hour of anguish Christ met and overcame all the horrors that Satan, "the prince of this world," could inflict.

—James E. Talmage[14]

In our very mortal human nature, we desperately want to be able to measure the Lord's suffering in Gethsemane—to somehow quantify it in terms we can understand, to put it against the familiar, to hold it in a way that allows for inspection. But all our efforts are frustrated, because what the Savior underwent in Gethsemane transcends any measuring stick or scale we could possibly use to enumerate it. With all of the Christian world, we stand amazed that He bore the terrible consequences of our collective sins—but, even more, voices from the dust tell us that He added to that burden all our pains, sorrows, and sicknesses as well (see Alma 7:11–12).

He lived a perfect life, and out of His incomprehensible love for us, He chose to enter our very imperfect lives by taking upon Himself all that made us insufficient.

The place He chose was a small, secluded grove of olive trees, partway up the slope of what was called Mount Olivet, where He and His disciples had often gone to ponder, meditate, and pray. It was a place well known to Him, a place where He had experienced great comfort and the support of close associates. We can only imagine that perhaps He hoped to find there the remnants of some unseen consolation.

The word *Gethsemane* comes from the Hebrew words for "oil" and "press"; indeed, nestled among the trees there stood a small olive press. The only way to extract the healing oil from the olives was with the enormous weight of the press, first bruising and then crushing the ripened fruit. In a similar way unfathomable to us, the only way to extract the Savior's atoning blood was to bruise and crush Him under the enormous weight of our collective sins. The prophet Isaiah illustrates it well: "he was wounded for our transgressions, he was bruised for our iniquities" (Isa. 53:5). Millennia-old trees still standing in the garden today are gnarled and twisted, as though mute witnesses of His unspeakable agony.

Having made their way along the deep ravine of the Kidron Valley, the Savior and

And he will take upon him their infirmities, . . . that he may know according to the flesh how to succor his people according to their infirmities.

DOCTRINE AND COVENANTS 25:4

His Eleven climbed the steep highway that skirted past the quiet orchard of olive trees. Near its entrance, He left eight of His disciples with the instruction, "Sit ye here, while I go and pray yonder" (Matt. 26:36). Then with what the gospel writers describe as a sorrowful countenance—so heavy that Talmage tells us it surprised even the Savior Himself[15]—He went into the garden with Peter,

James, and John, telling these, His best friends, "My soul is exceeding sorrowful, even unto death: tarry ye here, and watch with me" (Matt. 26:38).

A few steps further into the orchard, perhaps beyond another tree or two, He "fell on his face, and prayed" (Matt. 26:39). Among the first words to escape His lips, and the only ones heard

by His waiting disciples, were the pleading cry that at once revealed both His desperation and His determination: "O my Father, if it be possible, let this cup pass from me: nevertheless not as I will, but as thou wilt" (Matt. 26:39). We hear in His humble supplication no hesitation, no change of heart, no desire to withdraw from a mission that was His from the dawn of eternity. What we do hear is His utter understanding of the terrible agony that awaited Him.

There are no mortal witnesses to what happened next. As they had on the Mount of Transfiguration, the three disciples, overcome by weariness, slept. Returning to His three disciples in what Talmage describes as "agony of soul,"[16] and finding them sleeping, Jesus awakened Peter and asked, "What, could ye not watch with me one hour?" (Matt. 26:40). We can only imagine the embarrassment of Peter, who only hours earlier had announced his desire to go with the Savior even unto prison or death. But again we see evidence of the Savior's love and tenderness when He gave His slumbering disciples all benefit of the doubt: "the spirit indeed is willing, but the flesh is weak" (Matt. 26:41). Not only was the hour late, but the events that had already transpired that night had undoubtedly exacted a heavy emotional toll on men who were struggling to understand all that was unfolding.

We know he suffered, both body and spirit, more than it is possible for man to suffer, except it be unto death.

BRUCE R. MCCONKIE, "THE PURIFYING POWER OF GETHSEMANE," *ENSIGN*, MAY 1985

Undoubtedly sensing the dangers that lurked beyond the grove of olive trees, the Savior told His disciples to "Watch and pray, that ye enter not into temptation" (Matt. 26:41). According to Talmage, "The admonition to the apostles to pray at that time lest they be led into temptation may have been prompted by the exigencies of the hour, under which, if left to themselves, they would be tempted to prematurely desert their Lord."[17]

Again the Lord retreated, and again He pleaded with the Father in agony. As Talmage tells it, "Returning a second time He found those whom He had so sorrowfully requested to watch with Him sleeping again, 'for their eyes were heavy'; and when awakened they were embarrassed or ashamed so that they wist not what to say. A third time He went to His lonely vigil and individual struggle, and was heard to implore the Father with the same words of yearning entreaty. Luke tells us that 'there appeared an angel unto him from heaven, strengthening him'; but not even the presence of this super-earthly visitant could dispel the awful anguish of His soul. 'And being in an agony he prayed more earnestly: and his sweat was as it were great drops of blood falling to the ground.'"[18]

The Savior claimed each of us as His own, for it is our names that were on His lips as He writhed in unspeakable agony.

To more fully appreciate His sacrifice, we must realize that the angel strengthened Him—perhaps cradled for a time His battered and spent body—but did not deliver Him. We must realize that this man, the very Son of God, had the power to summon legions of angels, to seek their deliverance, but He did not. He trod the winepress alone.

It occurs to us that even before the angel appeared, the Savior was not really alone in the garden. In addition to the incalculable anguish of bearing the sins of the world, Jesus was engaged in a battle unprecedented in its terror: Lucifer, who has waged war on all of us, fought with all his might to prevent the Savior from performing the Atonement—for without it, we would all be his. Instead, the Savior claimed each of us as His own, for it is our names that were on His lips as He writhed in unspeakable agony.

"Every muscle of the Savior, every virtue, every spiritual reservoir that could be called upon would be summoned in the struggle," wrote Elder Tad R. Callister. "No doubt there was an exhaustion of all energies, a straining of all faculties, an exercise of all powers. Only then, when seemingly all had been spent, would the forces of evil abandon their posts and retreat in horrible defeat. . . . The Great Deliverer [had] rescued us. . . . But, oh, what a battle! What wounds! What love! What cost!"[19] It is a cost that injects itself into every minute of our lives. "In the hours of gladness," wrote Truman G. Madsen, "should our cup run o'er, let us remember that to make that possible, a cup—the bitterest of cups—must have been drunk."[20]

As the events unfolded, says Talmage, "Peter had had a glimpse of the darksome road which he had professed himself so ready to tread; and the brothers James and John knew now better than before how unprepared they were to drink of the cup which the Lord would drain to its dregs."[21]

For a period of three or four hours the Savior suffered in a torment we can't begin to comprehend. "Hence His profound grief, His indescribable anguish, His overpowering torture," wrote President John Taylor, "all experienced in the submission to the eternal fiat of Jehovah and the requirements of an inexorable law."[22] His experience on the garden floor would have killed any mere mortal—but, of course, this was no mere mortal. His

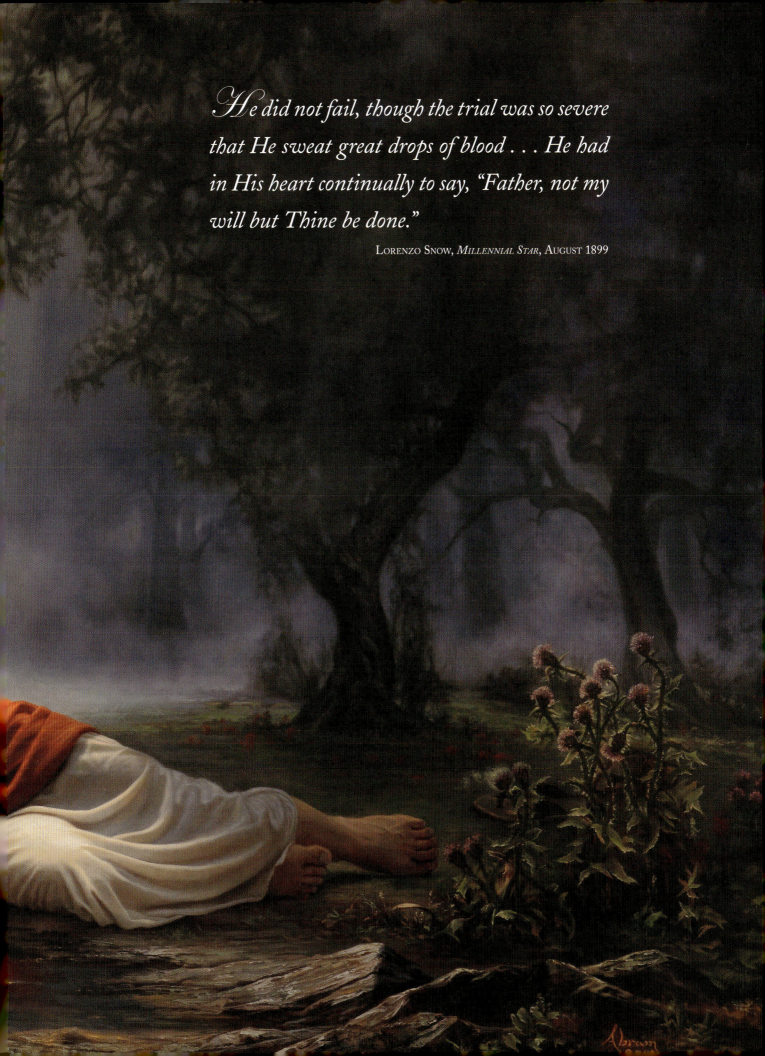

> *He did not fail, though the trial was so severe that He sweat great drops of blood . . . He had in His heart continually to say, "Father, not my will but Thine be done."*
>
> Lorenzo Snow, *Millennial Star*, August 1899

life could not be taken from Him; He had to voluntarily give it up. And in some way incomprehensible to the rest of us, He knew His sacrifice was not yet finished.

In the next hour, the disciples who stood watch would hear the approach of the soldiers. Then would come the betraying kiss, the arrest, and finally the scene in which all eleven disciples fled, forsaking the Lord. "It is possible," says Talmage, "that had any of the Eleven been apprehended with Jesus and made to share the cruel abuse and torturing humiliation of the next few hours, their faith might have failed them, relatively immature and untried as it then was."[23] And still, the atoning sacrifice would not be finished. But even with what lay ahead, He had endured to immense proportions in the awful calculation of the garden. He had fought the good fight, and He held the hard-won victory tenaciously within His broken hands.

"From the terrible conflict in Gethsemane, Christ emerged a victor," declared Talmage. "Though in the dark tribulation of that fearful hour He had pleaded that the bitter cup be removed from His lips, the request, however oft repeated, was always conditional; the accomplishment of the Father's will was never lost sight of as the Son's supreme desire. The further agony of the night, and the cruel inflictions that awaited Him on the morrow, to culminate in the frightful tortures of the cross, could not exceed the bitter anguish through which He had successfully passed."[24]

For behold, I, God, have suffered these things for all, that they might not suffer if they would repent; . . . which suffering caused myself, even God, the greatest of all, to tremble because of pain, and to bleed at every pore, and to suffer both body and spirit—and would that I might not drink the bitter cup, and shrink—Nevertheless, glory be to the Father; and I partook and finished my preparations unto the children of men.

D&C 19:16–19

THE *T*RIAL

Jesus stood convicted of the most heinous offense known in Jewry. However unjustly, He had been pronounced guilty of blasphemy by the supreme tribunal of the nation. . . . The high-priestly court . . . decided that Jesus was worthy of death, and so certified when they handed Him over to Pilate. In their excess of malignant hate, Israel's judges abandoned their Lord to the wanton will of the attendant varlets, who heaped upon Him every indignity their brutish instincts could suggest. They spurted their foul spittle into His face; and then, having blindfolded Him, amused themselves by smiting Him again and again. . . . The miscreant crowd mocked Him, and railed upon Him with jeers and taunts, and branded themselves as blasphemers in fact.

—James E. Talmage[25]

With the agonies of the garden behind Him, Jesus of Nazareth was arrested, bound, and taken captive to be interrogated before the chief priests, scribes, and elders. Much has been theorized about the trial that ensued; many have suggested that it was on numerous counts illegal—that the Savior was not given due considerations that were His under either Jewish or Roman law. No matter. The fact that Jesus was to be convicted on some charge—and was to be put to death as a result—had already been determined by the priestly judges before He was ever bound over to them.

Peter, who had followed the soldiers from afar as they traveled the road to Jerusalem from the garden, had secured admittance to the palace of Caiaphas, where the condemned Lord first stood before the Sanhedrin. But Peter, shrouded by the cover of night, remained below—sitting "with the servants, to see the end" (Matt. 26:58). Twice recognized as a friend of Jesus by two women among the crowd, he twice denied the charge—uttering the second time the oath, "I do not know the man" (Matt. 26:72).

An hour or so later, gathered with others at an open fire in the palace courtyard where they huddled against the evening chill, Peter was openly asked by a servant of the high priest, "Did not I see thee in the garden with him?" (John 18:26). With a curse on his lips, Peter vehemently maintained, "I know not the man" (Matt. 26:74). No sooner had "the last profane falsehood left his lips," says Talmage, than "the clear notes of a crowing cock broke upon his ears, and the remembrance of his Lord's prediction welled up in his mind. Trembling in wretched realization of his perfidious cowardice, he turned from the crowd and met the gaze of the suffering Christ, who from the midst of the insolent mob looked into the face of His boastful, yet loving but weak apostle. Hastening from the palace, Peter went out into the night, weeping bitterly."[26]

During the few hours that remained to Him in mortality, Talmage wrote, the Savior

44

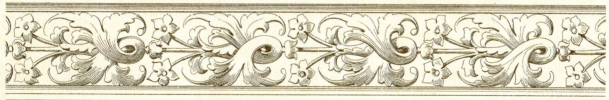

And immediately, while he yet spake, the cock crew. And the Lord turned, and looked upon Peter. And Peter remembered the word of the Lord....

Luke 22:60-61

"would be in the hands of the Gentiles, betrayed and delivered up by His own."[27] It was for them, in very fact, that the Savior had endured the agonies of Gethsemane—for them, as for all of us, that He paid the terrible price.

The next morning, the Great Sanhedrin again assembled to hold the second trial, mandatory for any prisoner sentenced to death. Of all His disciples, only one—Luke, the physician—was with Him. In their scramble to convict Him, "all the chief priests and elders of the people took counsel against Jesus to put him to death" (Matt. 27:1). At that point, they "bound Jesus, and carried him away, and delivered him to Pilate" (Mark 15:1). Because the Jews would not enter the house of a Gentile during Passover, to avoid risking exposure to leavened bread, Pilate was forced to come outside to hear their charges. What twisted irony in the fact that they who feared the proximity of leaven would instead be thirsting for innocent blood.[28]

It was Pontius Pilate—governor of Rome, procurator of Judea, Samaria, and Idumea—who had to declare the death sentence, for by law no Jewish tribunal had authority to inflict such a punishment. It is part of history, made clear in sacred writ, that Pilate resisted. To the first appeal by the Jews, he declared, "I find in him no fault at all" (John 18:38). When Herod also failed to find in Jesus a punishable offense—though he and his men made sport of Christ and mocked Him—the determined Jews returned again to Pilate.

Again the governor recoiled: "Ye have brought this man unto me, as one that perverteth the people: and, behold, I, having examined him before you, have found no fault in this man touching those things whereof ye accuse him: No, nor yet Herod: . . . nothing worthy of death is done unto him. I will therefore chastise him, and release him" (Luke 23:14–16).

Calling on the tradition of pardoning and releasing one prisoner at Passover, Pilate made yet a third attempt to free the Savior. Instead, the crowd demanded that he pardon Barabbas—whose name literally means "son of the father." How ironic that the true Son of the Father was detained while Barabbas, a murderer also found guilty of sedition, was set free. Sorely troubled, Pilate called

> *The instrument of punishment was a whip of many thongs, loaded with metal and edged with jagged pieces of bone.*
>
> JAMES E. TALMAGE, *JESUS THE CHRIST*

for water and washed his hands before the multitude in a symbolic act of disclaiming responsibility for what was about to happen. "I am innocent of the blood of this just person: see ye to it" (Matt. 27:24). From the crowd assembled arose the cry of self-condemnation: "His blood be on us, and on our children" (Matt. 27:25).

Pilate released Barabbas, and gave Jesus to the soldiers to be scourged. "Scourging," explains Talmage, "was a frightful preliminary to death on the cross. The instrument of punishment was a whip of many thongs, loaded with metal and edged with jagged pieces of bone. Instances are of record in which the condemned died under the lash and so escaped the horrors of living crucifixion." After being scourged, His flesh ripped and torn, Jesus was "given over to the half-savage soldiers for their amusement. . . . They stripped Jesus of His outer raiment, and placed upon Him a purple robe. Then with a sense of fiendish realism they platted a crown of thorns, and placed it about the Sufferer's brows; a reed was put into His right hand as a royal scepter; and, as they bowed in mockery of homage, they saluted Him with: 'Hail, King of the Jews!' Snatching away the reed or rod, they brutally

> *They platted a crown of thorns, and placed it about the Sufferer's brows; a reed was put into His right hand as a royal scepter....*
>
> JAMES E. TALMAGE, *JESUS THE CHRIST*

smote Him with it upon the head, driving the cruel thorns into His quivering flesh; they slapped Him with their hands, and spat upon Him in vile and vicious abandonment."[29]

Yet again Pilate intervened. Putting a stop to the barbarous scene, he once more brought Jesus in front of the teeming crowd—hoping, we imagine, that the sight of the Savior in such torment would soften their hearts. But the crowd was not to be subdued. Once again proclaiming the Savior's innocence, Pilate relented to the vehemence of those who demanded the crucifixion of Jesus. Pronouncing the death sentence, "Take ye him, and crucify him," Pilate added his solemn testimony: "for I find no fault in him" (John 19:6). In one final attempt, he asked those gathered, "Shall I crucify your King?" to which the chief priests answered, "We have no king but Caesar" (John 19:15).

"With this cry Judaism was, in the person of its representatives, guilty of denial of God, of blasphemy, of apostasy," wrote biblical scholar Alfred Edersheim. "It committed suicide; and ever since has its dead body been carried in show from land to land, and from century to century,—to be dead and to remain dead, till He come a second time, who is the resurrection and the life."[30]

And what of Judas, whose betrayal had put in motion the trial and fatal sentence? As preparations were being made for the crucifixion, he implored the rulers to take back the wage they had paid him. Perhaps he now hoped for a reversal of the sentence, but none such was to be found. Crying in despair, he said, "I have sinned, in that I have betrayed the innocent blood," to which they responded with disgust, "What is that to us?" (Matt. 27:4).

"He had served their purpose; they had paid him his price; they wished never to look upon his face again; and pitilessly they flung him back into the haunted blackness of his maddened conscience," wrote Talmage. "Still clutching the bag of silver, the all too real remembrancer of his frightful sin, he rushed into the temple, penetrating even to the precincts of priestly reservation, and dashed the silver pieces upon the floor of the sanctuary. Then, under the goading impulse of his master, the devil, to whom he had become a bond-slave, body and soul, he went out and hanged himself."[31]

Barred from adding the tainted coin to the sacred treasury, the priests used the silver to

Now the greatest and most important single thing there is in eternity—the thing that transcends all others since the time of the creation of man and of the worlds—is the fact of the atoning sacrifice of Christ the Lord.

Bruce R. McConkie, "Behold the Condescension of God," *New Era*, December 1984

purchase a clay-yard, the tract of ground where Judas had hanged himself, which they set apart as *Aceldama*—"the field of blood"—a burial place for aliens, strangers, and pagans. The body of Judas was probably the first to be there interred.[32]

Listen to him who is the advocate with the Father, who is pleading your cause before him—

Saying: Father, behold the sufferings and death of him who did no sin, in whom thou wast well pleased; behold the blood of thy Son which was shed, the blood of him whom thou gavest that thyself might be glorified;

Wherefore, Father, spare these my brethren that believe on my name, that they may come unto me and have everlasting life.

D&C 45:3–5

THE CRUCIFIXION

The dominant note in all the railings and revilings, the ribaldry and mockery, with which the patient and submissive Christ was assailed while He hung . . . was that awful "If" hurled at Him by the devil's emissaries in the time of mortal agony. . . . That "If" was Satan's last shaft, keenly barbed and doubly envenomed, and it sped as with the fierce hiss of a viper. Was it possible in this the final and most dreadful stage of Christ's mission, to make Him doubt His divine Sonship, or, failing such, to taunt or anger the dying Savior into the use of His superhuman powers for personal relief or as an act of vengeance upon His tormentors? To achieve such a victory was Satan's desperate purpose. The shaft failed. Through taunts and derision, through blasphemous challenge and diabolical goading, the agonized Christ was silent.

—James E. Talmage[33]

The hurried preparations were made for a triple crucifixion: two convicted criminals, sentenced to the cross for robbery, were led forth to death at the same time as Jesus, who had been divested of His purple robe and wore only His own raiment. Because Roman custom called for public execution, the trio sentenced to death were to be crucified at Golgotha, atop a craggy cliff overlooking a well-traveled highway. Custom also called for the condemned to carry the cross upon which he was to suffer.

And so it was, as Talmage tells us, that "Jesus started on the way bearing His cross. The terrible strain of the preceding hours, the agony in Gethsemane, the barbarous treatment He had suffered in the palace of the high priest, . . . the frightful scourging under Pilate's order, the brutal treatment by the inhuman soldiery . . . had so weakened His physical organism that He moved by slowly under the burden of the cross."[34] The soldiers, impatient to be finished with their heinous chore, pressed into service a man named Simon, a native of Cyrene; traveling to Jerusalem from the country, he was compelled to carry the cross for Jesus, for no Roman or Jew would have voluntarily carried out such a disgraceful task.

The cortege made its way along the city streets, out through the portal of the massive wall, to the designated place beyond the city. Among the crowds who pressed to see this Jesus travel to His death, not a man lifted His voice in protest or sorrow. Only a handful of women, scattered among the bloodthirsty throng, cried out in grief-stricken lamentation.

And he bearing his cross went forth into a place called the place of a skull, which is called in the Hebrew Golgotha.

JOHN 19:17

Reaching Golgotha, "the place of a skull," the officers immediately moved to carry out the execution. These had likely become callous, since killing was their trade. Even so, before affixing the condemned to the cross, they complied with the Jewish custom to offer the condemned a narcotic drink of sour wine or vinegar mingled with myrrh and other painkilling ingredients.

But when the cup was offered to Jesus, He refused it. He was determined to meet death with, as Talmage tells us, "faculties alert and mind unclouded."[35]

And so it was that the sound of steel against steel rang through the gathering dusk as great spikes were nailed through the Savior's hands and feet. The heavy cross upon which He was nailed

was pushed upward and then dropped into the prepared hole. At the top, above Jesus' head, was affixed a title—*THIS IS JESUS THE KING OF THE JEWS* (Matt. 27:37)—inscribed in three languages: Greek, Latin, and Hebrew. His was the center cross, positioned between those of the two convicted robbers.

As He hung in awful agony, the four soldiers at His feet distributed among themselves His clothing, according to Roman rule. There remained His quality-crafted coat, woven without seam; not wanting to ruin it by tearing it in pieces, the soldiers cast lots to determine who would take it away from the crucifixion. In their simple act the Gospel writers saw fulfillment of the Psalmist's vision: "They part my garments among them, and cast lots upon my vesture" (Ps. 22:18). Seeing at once the heartlessness of the soldiers' cruel capacities, the Savior made the first of His utterances from the cross: "Father, forgive them; for they know not what they do" (Luke 23:34). It was a plea far-reaching in the immensity of its scope, extending eternities beyond the palming of a simple carpenter's coat.

With a duty to guard the cross until death relieved its victim, the soldiers soon grew restless with their obligation and turned to deriding and mocking Jesus, issuing what Talmage calls the devil-inspired challenge, "If thou be the king of the Jews, save thyself" (Luke 23:37). They were joined by mobs of passersby, who dared Him—a man who destroyed the temple

The gift of His life was exactly that: a gift, given voluntarily—something no band of men . . . could take from Him.

and then rebuilt it in three days—to come down from the cross and save Himself (see Mark 15:29–30). Ringleaders of the tormenters were the inhumane members of the Sanhedrin, priests who esteemed themselves greater than all, who gloated, "He saved others; himself he cannot save. Let Christ the King of Israel descend now from the cross, that we may see and believe" (Mark 15:31–32).

Mired in a spiritual wasteland, none understood the truth: that He could indeed have descended from the cross and saved Himself without the minutest difficulty. That He could have summoned legions of angels to lift Him from the cross, bringing exquisite relief from the agonizing pain. That the gift of His life was exactly that: a gift, given voluntarily—something that no band of men, equipped with spears and hammers and steel spikes, could take from Him.

At last softened by the Savior's uncomplaining attitude, one of the thieves beside Him proclaimed of Jesus, "this man has done nothing amiss" (Luke 23:41). Gazing at the Savior, he then uttered, "Lord, remember me when thou comest into thy kingdom" (Luke 23:43).

Jesus looked down with immense compassion upon His mother, who stood weeping next to His beloved disciple.

Undoubtedly touched by the first tentative sign of support in His mean condition, the Savior looked with love upon his companion and gave a promise He alone could make: "Verily I say unto thee, To day shalt thou be with me in paradise" (Luke 23:43).

Sprinkled among the soldiers and priests who mocked and scorned the Savior were a number of those who supported Him. Only one of the Twelve—John, the beloved Apostle, evangelist, and Revelator—was recorded as being there to sustain his Master. We know too of at least three women who wept in anguish at the foot of the cross: Mary, the Savior's mother; her sister Mary, the wife of Cleophas; and Mary Magdalene (see John 19:25).

Somehow miraculously putting aside His own agony, Jesus looked down with immense compassion upon His mother, who stood weeping next to His beloved disciple. Commending her to the care of one He trusted without hesitation, He directed, "Woman, behold thy son!" (John 19:26), and to John, "Behold thy mother!" (John 19:27). The disciple tenderly led the grief-stricken Mary away from her dying Son and "from that hour . . . took her unto his own home" (John 19:27).

We know very little of what else happened during the hours the Savior suffered at Golgotha. We know that He was nailed to the cross between nine and ten in the morning that Friday, and that by noontide a black darkness had spread over the entire land, a gloom that lasted for three hours and that was engineered by divine power—"a fitting sign of the earth's deep mourning over the impending death of her Creator,"[36] wrote Talmage.

Regarding the approximate six hours He hung in anguish at Golgotha, we know few precise details. "Of the mortal agony through which the Lord passed while upon the cross, the Gospel-scribes are reverently reticent,"[37] Talmage says. We do know some generalities that can certainly be applied to the Savior's experience. "Death by crucifixion was at once the most lingering and most painful of all forms of execution," Talmage wrote. "The victim lived in ever increasing torture, generally for many hours, sometimes for days. The spikes so cruelly driven through hands and feet penetrated and crushed sensitive nerves and quivering tendons, yet inflicted no mortal wound. The welcome relief of death came through the exhaustion caused

We believe absolutely in Jesus Christ, that He was the Son of God, and that He did come to the earth . . . to die as the Redeemer of mankind, on the cross.

HEBER J. GRANT, "ARTICLES OF FAITH EXPLAINED," *DESERET NEWS*, SEPTEMBER 1938

by intense and unremitting pain, through localized inflammation and congestion of organs incident to the strained and unnatural position of the body."³⁸

But the agonies of the crucifixion itself were only the beginning in the case of this, the Savior, Lord, and Redeemer. For while He endured the physical agonies designed to kill Him, Jesus of Nazareth once again went through extremities incomprehensible to us.

"At the ninth hour, or about three in the afternoon, a loud voice, surpassing the most anguished cry of physical suffering issued from the central cross, rending the dreadful darkness," wrote Talmage. "It was the voice of the Christ: *'Eloi, Eloi, lama sabachthani? which is, being interpreted, My God, my God, why hast thou forsaken me?'* What mind of man can fathom the significance of that awful cry? It seems, that in addition to the fearful suffering incident to crucifixion, the agony of Gethsemane had recurred, intensified beyond human power to endure. In that bitterest hour the dying Christ was alone, alone in most terrible reality. That the supreme sacrifice of the Son might be consummated in all its fulness, the Father seems to have withdrawn the support of His immediate Presence, leaving to the Savior of men the glory of complete victory over the forces of sin and death."³⁹

"Groaning beneath this concentrated load, this intense, incomprehensible pressure, this terrible exaction of Divine justice," wrote John Taylor, ". . . seemingly forsaken by His God, on the cross He bowed beneath the accumulated load, and cried out in anguish, 'My God, my God, why has thou forsaken me!'"⁴⁰

Forsaken? No. But as Elder Melvin J. Ballard wrote,

> . . . in that hour I think I can see our dear Father behind the veil looking upon these dying struggles until even he could not endure it any longer; and, like the mother who bids farewell to her dying child, has to be taken out of the room, so as not to look upon the last struggles, so he bowed his head, and hid in some part of the universe, his great heart almost breaking for the love that he had for his Son. Oh, in that moment when he might have saved his Son, I thank him and praise him that he did not fail us. . . . I rejoice that he did not interfere, and that his

This extreme suffering—which was beyond the power of mortal man either to accomplish or endure—was undertaken because of the great love which the Father and the Son had for all mankind. . . .

Joseph Fielding Smith, *Doctrines of Salvation*, 1954–56

love for us made it possible for him to endure to look upon the sufferings of his Son and give him finally to us, our Savior and our Redeemer.⁴¹

Knowing His sacrifice had been accepted by the Father, and assured that His mission in the flesh had been gloriously consummated, the Lord and Savior Jesus Christ exclaimed in a loud voice of holy triumph: "It is finished" (John 19:30). Bowing His head in reverence and relief, He addressed the Father, saying, "Father, into thy hands I commend my spirit" (Luke 23:46). At that, say the Gospel writers, he gave up the ghost.

"Jesus the Christ was dead," wrote Talmage. "His life had not been taken from Him except as He had willed to permit. Sweet and welcome as would have been the relief of death in any of the earlier stages of His suffering from Gethsemane to the cross, He lived until all things were accomplished as had been appointed."⁴²

As the Sabbath and paschal holy day approached, Jewish officials pleaded with the Roman soldiers to break the legs of the three condemned—a violent assault that brought immediate death—so that the bodies could be lowered from the crosses before the Sabbath. The legs of the two thieves were broken with short, heavy clubs called cudgels. But finding the Savior already dead, the soldiers did not break His bones, a fulfillment of prophecy. One of the soldiers, to make sure He was already dead, thrust a spear into His side, leaving a wound large enough to accommodate a man's hand. John, witnessing the outpouring of blood and water—likely from a ruptured heart—bore specific testimony to the fact that the scriptures had been fulfilled.

We know of the tumult that followed the Savior's death. Violent earthquakes disrupted

the rocks of the mighty hills, and graves were opened. The veil of the temple was rent from top to bottom, exposing the Holy of Holies to common gaze. The Roman soldiers, wrote Talmage, "had probably witnessed many deaths on the cross, but never before had they seen a man apparently die of his own volition, and able to cry in a loud voice at the moment of dissolution. . . . so impressed [was] the centurion that he prayed to God, and solemnly declared: 'Certainly this was a righteous man.' Others joined in fearsome averment: 'Truly this was the Son of God.'"[43]

To prevent the Savior's body being cast into the common grave of executed criminals, Joseph of Arimathea—a good and just man of wealth and influence who had been a silent disciple of the Savior—asked for the Savior's body and offered his own tomb in a nearby garden. Then came Nicodemus, who brought "a hundredweight"[44] of myrrh and aloe, restricted to the wealthy for use in anointing and embalming. With the rapid approach of the Sabbath, the two revering disciples worked in haste to prepare the body for burial. Then, wrapping the body in clean linen, they laid it "in a new sepulchre, hewn in the rock. . . . the door of the sepulchre was closed, a large stone was rolled against it; and thus laid away the body was left to rest."[45] Roman soldiers were dispatched to guard the tomb, lest the Savior's disciples come and take His body to support spurious claims that He had risen.

The Savior's life was, in His own words, finished. But still to come was the glorious final chapter, the life-giving conclusion to the Atonement. As His disciples reverenced His body and laid it in the tomb, the suffering in Gethsemane and on the cross caused our sins to "cease to be ours," wrote Talmage, "and as far as the justice of God is concerned, we never committed them. Through the Atonement, we are not merely forgiven—we are rendered innocent once again. . . ."[46]

For, behold, the Lord your Redeemer suffered death in the flesh; wherefore he suffered the pain of all men, that all men might repent and come unto him.

D&C 18:11

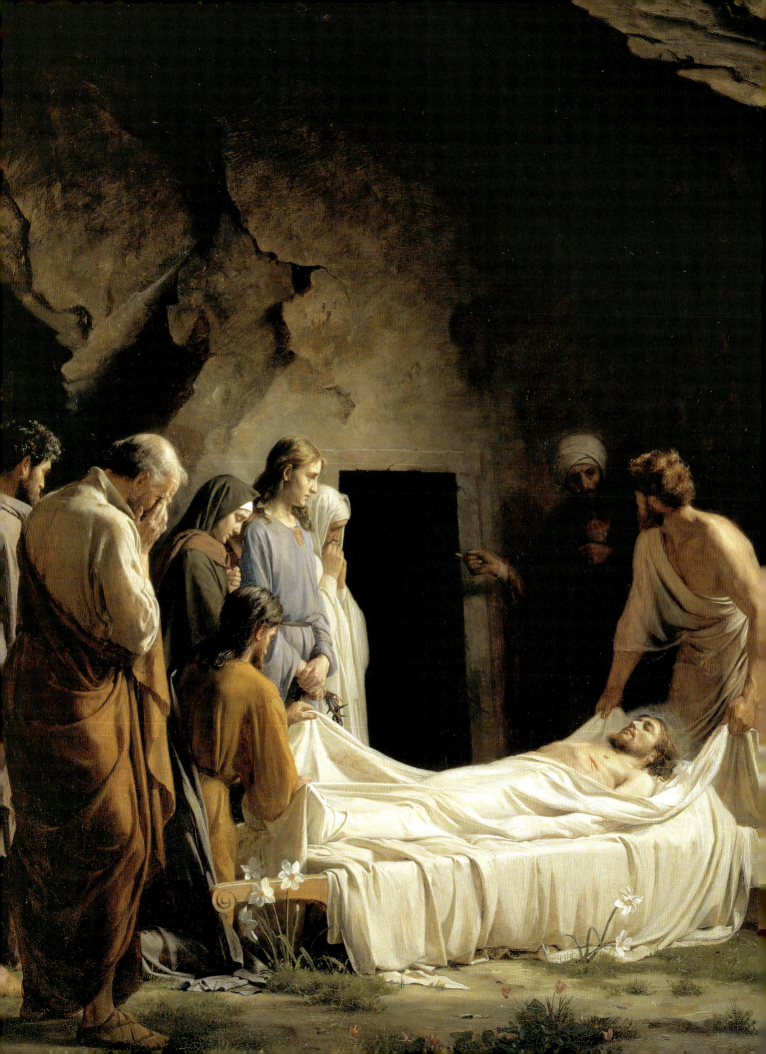

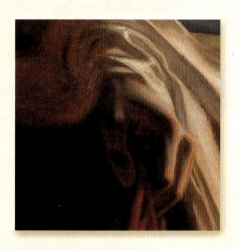

THE RESURRECTION

    While it was yet dark, the earth began to quake; an angel of the Lord descended in glory, rolled back the massive stone from the portal of the tomb, and sat upon it. His countenance was brilliant as the lightning, and his raiment was as the driven snow for whiteness. The soldiers, paralyzed with fear, fell to the earth as dead men. When they had partially recovered from their fright, they fled from the place in terror. Even the rigor of Roman discipline, which decreed summary death to every soldier who deserted his post, could not deter them. Moreover, there was nothing left for them to guard; the seal of authority had been broken, the sepulchre was open, and empty.

—James E. Talmage[47]

As the earliest tendrils of light began to touch Jerusalem that Sunday morning, a small band of faithful women led by Mary Magdalene made their way to the tomb where the Savior's body had been laid. They had seen the haste with which Joseph and Nicodemus had prepared the corpse that Friday eve, pressed by the impending setting of the sun that signaled the arrival of the Sabbath. Now they made their way along the road to the garden, still deserted in the early-morning hour, bearing spices and ointments with which to more thoroughly embalm the body of their Lord.

Arriving at the tomb, they found not a sentinel of Roman soldiers, but instead a single angel. The stone had been rolled away from the entrance of the sepulchre, which stood empty. Having witnessed for themselves the vile persecutions of their Lord, it is no wonder that they feared His body had been taken by malefactors.

But theirs was to be divine assurance, a first witness to the fulfillment of the Savior's promise, when the angel told them, "Fear not ye: for I know that ye seek Jesus, which was crucified. He is not here: for he is risen, as he said. Come, see the place where the Lord lay. And go quickly, and tell his disciples that he is risen from the dead; and, behold, he goeth before you into Galilee; there shall ye see him: lo, I have told you" (Matt. 28:5–7).

Astonished—and likely somewhat fearful—the women fled, Mary Magdalene being the first to find the disciples. "Then she runneth," we are told, "and cometh to Simon Peter, and to the other disciple, whom Jesus loved, and saith unto them, They have taken away the Lord out of the sepulchre, and we know not where they have laid him" (John 20:2). It seems, writes Talmage, that she "had failed to comprehend the gladsome meaning of the angel's proclamation 'He is risen, as he

He is not here: for he is risen, as he said. Come, see the place where the Lord lay. And go quickly, and tell his disciples that he is risen from the dead....

MATTHEW 28:6–7

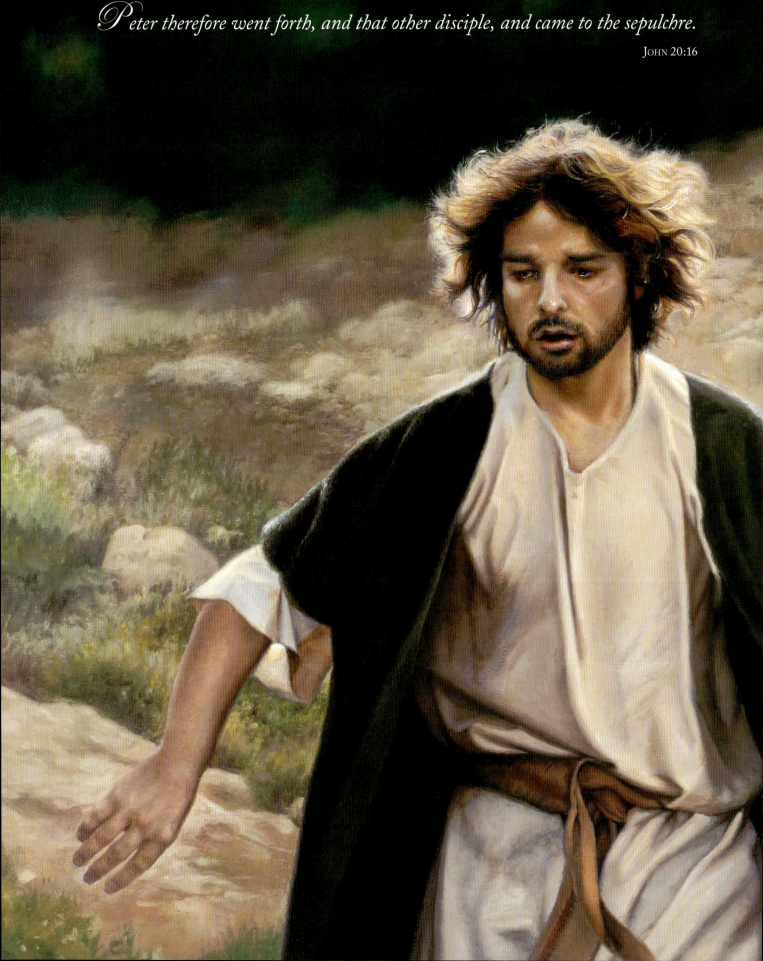

Jesus saith unto her, Mary. She turned herself, and saith unto him, Rabboni; which is to say, Master.

John 20:16

said'; in her agony of love and grief she remembered only the words 'He is not here,' the truth of which had been so forcefully impressed by her own hasty glance at the open and tenantless tomb."[48]

We can only imagine the raw emotion that seized Peter and that other disciple—almost certainly John—as they ran together to the sepulchre. Entering the tomb, they saw the linen graveclothes and, lying by itself, the napkin that had been placed around the Savior's head. It was, indeed, as He had said: He had risen.

Mary, who had remained outside the tomb weeping, entered it again once Peter and John left to carry the news to the other Apostles. There, in addition to the abandoned linen graveclothes, she saw two angels in white—one sitting at the head and the other at the foot of the place where the body of Jesus had lain. Tenderly, they asked of her, "Woman, why weepest thou?" In her devastating sorrow, she could but reply in what was an entire volume of pathos, "Because they have taken away my Lord, and I know not where they have laid him" (John 20:13).

Turning from the tomb, she became aware of another personage, standing outside the sepulchre. With tender sympathy not unlike that of the angels, He asked, "Woman, why weepest thou? whom seekest thou?" Scarcely looking up at who she assumed to be the caretaker of the garden, she pleaded, "Sir, if thou have borne him hence, tell me where thou hast laid him, and I will take him away" (John 20:15). If He had been dispossessed of the borrowed tomb, this woman was prepared to provide another.

What happened next stands in history as a singular event. We know it was Jesus to whom she spoke—though she knew it not. As Talmage writes, "One word from His living lips changed her agonized grief into ecstatic joy. 'Jesus saith unto her, Mary.' The voice, the

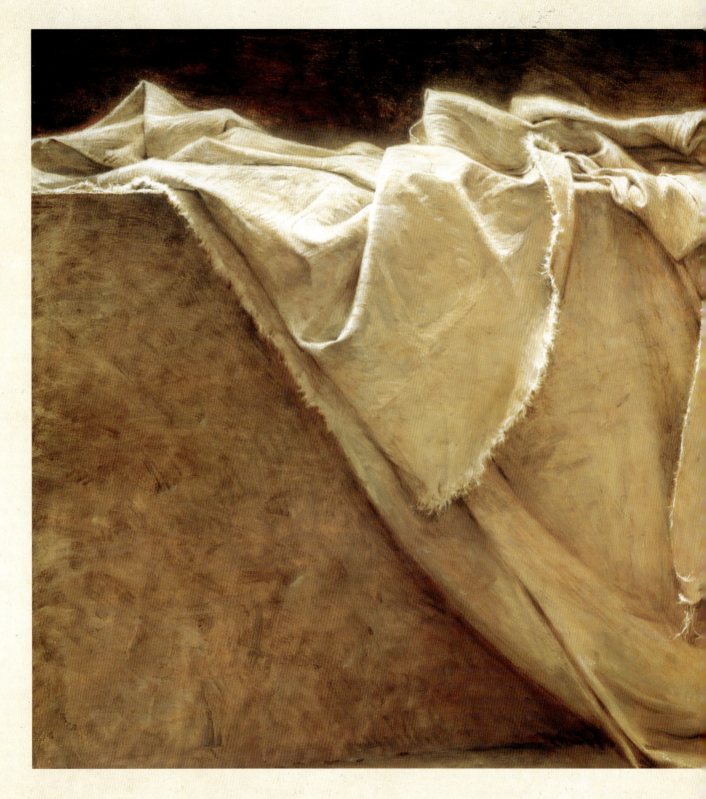

tone, the tender accent she had heard and loved in the earlier days lifted her from the despairing depths into which she had sunk. She turned, and saw the Lord. In a transport of joy she reached out her arms to embrace Him, uttering only the endearing and worshipful word, 'Rabboni,' meaning My beloved Master."[49]

Jesus restrained her, saying, "Touch me not; for I am not yet ascended to my Father: but go to my brethren, and say unto them, I ascend unto my Father, and your Father; and to my God, and your God" (John 20:17).

A woman, then, was given the honor of being the first mortal to see a resurrected soul. We

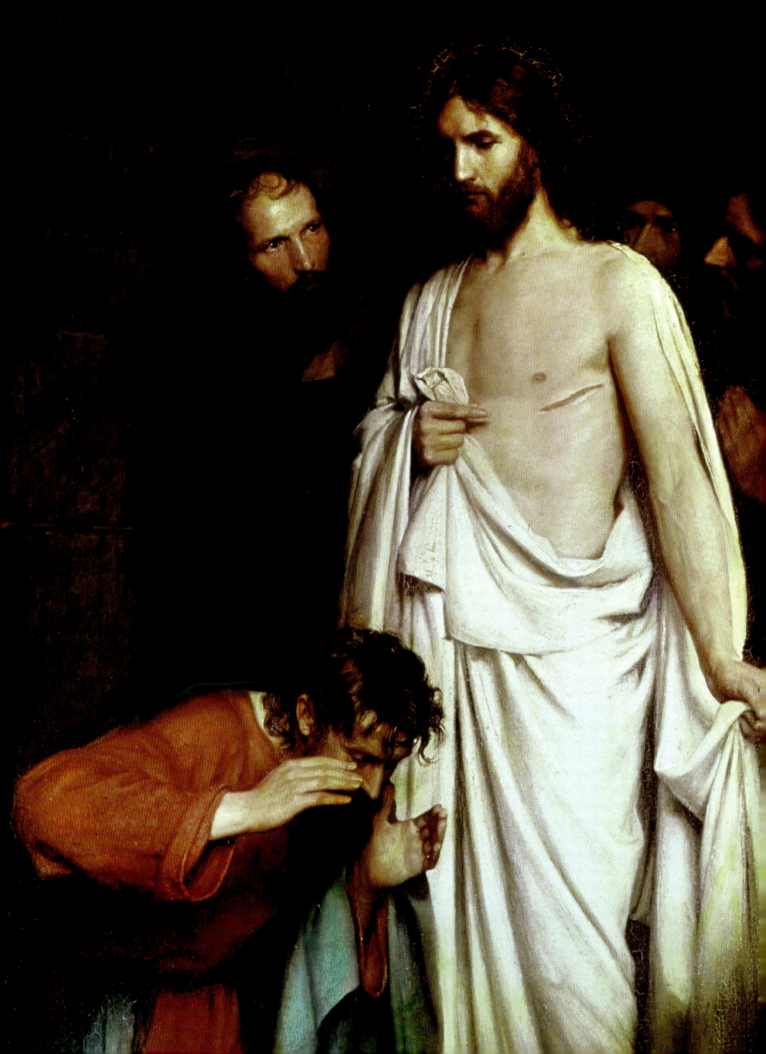

know that during the next few hours, Christ manifested Himself to other chosen women as well. But when they testified to the Apostles, their words "seemed to them as idle tales, and they believed them not" (Luke 24:11). To these earnest and faithful Apostles came words that seemed remote, beyond the scope of possibility—that a person once dead was now alive, with a body of flesh and bones that could be seen and felt. They had never known such a thing.

Yet they would know it now. One by one, the Eleven—even Thomas, who was invited to "reach hither thy hand, and thrust it into my side: and be not faithless, but believing" (John 20:27)—saw for themselves the resurrected Lord near Jerusalem, at the Sea of Tiberias, on a mountain in Galilee. Others saw Him, too—disciples on the road to Emmaus, and a crowd numbered at five hundred.

How significant is Christ's Resurrection? "Without the Resurrection, the gospel of Jesus Christ becomes a litany of wise sayings and seemingly unexplainable miracles—but sayings and miracles with no ultimate triumph," wrote President Howard W. Hunter. "No, the ultimate triumph is in the ultimate miracle: for the first time in the history of mankind, one who was dead raised himself into living immorality. He *was* the Son of God, the Son of our immortal Father in Heaven, and his triumph over physical and spiritual death is the good news every Christian tongue should

speak. The eternal truth is that Jesus Christ arose from the grave and was the firstfruits of the Resurrection."[50]

Forty days after His Resurrection, the Savior met with the Eleven in one last sacred interview near Bethany on the Mount of Olives. Delivering there a sacred commission to "Go ye therefore, and teach all nations" (Matt. 28:19), Jesus of Nazareth—now a resurrected, glorious being—promised to be with them always, even unto the end of the world.

Talmage tells us that the Lord then "lifted up His hands, and blessed them; and while yet He spake, He rose from their midst, and they looked upon Him as He ascended until a cloud received Him out of their sight. . . . Worshipfully and with great joy the apostles returned to Jerusalem. . . . The Lord's ascension was accomplished; it was as truly a literal departure of a material Being as His resurrection had been an actual return of His spirit to His own corporeal body, theretofore dead. With the world abode and yet abides the glorious promise, that Jesus the Christ, the same Being who ascended from Olivet in His immortalized body of flesh and bones, shall return, descending from the heavens, in similarly material form and substance."[51]

And so it was that the infinite Atonement, the greatest gift ever given, was complete. With it comes the opportunity for each of us to return to that Father who gave us life—to God, who is our home. Because of it comes the chance to inherit all that He has. And as a result of it, death and the grave must surrender us. We will live again, each and every one of us, through our association with the Savior and Redeemer of all mankind.

As verified in that second witness of Christ, "O how great the goodness of our God, who prepareth a way for our escape from the grasp of this awful monster; yea, that monster, death and hell, which I call the death of the body, and also the death of the spirit" (2 Ne. 9:10).

As President David O. McKay so beautifully put it, "To sincere believers in Christianity, to all who accept Christ as their Savior, his resurrection is not a symbolism but a reality. As Christ lived after death, so shall all men, each taking his place in the next world. . . . Because our Redeemer lives, so shall we."[52]

He is not here: for he is risen, as he said.

Matt. 28:6

Endnotes

1 James E. Talmage, *Jesus the Christ* (American Fork, UT: Covenant Communications, 2002), 1.
2 Bruce R. McConkie, "Once or Twice in a Thousand Years," *Ensign*, November 1975, 15.
3 *Jesus the Christ*, 2.
4 Ibid., 3.
5 Bruce R. McConkie, "A God Is Born," *Christmas Classics: A Treasury for Latter-day Saints* (Salt Lake City: Deseret Book Company, 1991), 121.
6 Hugh Nibley, "One of the Grand Constants in Nature," in Don E. Norton, ed., *Approaching Zion* (Salt Lake City and Provo, Utah: Deseret Book Company and FARMS, 1989), 603.
7 *Jesus the Christ*, 424.
8 Ibid., 419.
9 Ibid., 420.
10 Ibid., 421–422.
11 Ibid., 423.
12 Ibid., 426.
13 Ibid., 427.
14 Ibid., 428–429.
15 See *Jesus the Christ*, 428.
16 *Jesus the Christ*, 428.
17 Ibid.
18 Ibid.
19 Tad R. Callister, *The Infinite Atonement* (Salt Lake City: Deseret Book Company, 2000), 134.
20 Truman G. Madsen, *The Radiant Life* (Salt Lake City: Bookcraft, 1994). 16.
21 *Jesus the Christ*, 428.
22 John Taylor, *The Mediation and Atonement* (Salt Lake City: Deseret News Company, 1882), 149.
23 *Jesus the Christ*, 430.
24 Ibid., 429.
25 Ibid., 440.
26 Ibid., 442.
27 Ibid.
28 See *Jesus the Christ*, 443.
29 *Jesus the Christ*, 446–447.
30 Alfred Edersheim, *The Bible History Old Testament*, Vol. 2 (1890), 581.
31 *Jesus the Christ*, 448.
32 Ibid, 449.
33 Ibid., 460–461.
34 Ibid., 457–458.
35 Ibid., 459.
36 Ibid., 462.
37 Ibid.
38 Ibid., 459.
39 Ibid., 462.
40 *The Mediation and Atonement*, 149.
41 Bryant S. Hinckley, comp., *Sermons and Missionary Services of Melvin Joseph Ballard* (Salt Lake City: Deseret Book Company, 1949), 155.
42 *Jesus the Christ*, 462.
43 Ibid., 463.
44 Ibid., 464.
45 Ibid.
46 Stephen E. Robinson, *Believing Christ: The Parable of the Bicycle and Other Good News* (Salt Lake City: Deseret Book Company, 1992), 118.
47 *Jesus the Christ*, 475.
48 Ibid., 476.
49 Ibid., 477.
50 Howard W. Hunter, "An Apostle's Witness of the Resurrection," *Ensign*, May 1986, 15.
51 *Jesus the Christ*, 485.
52 David O. McKay, "Easter—and the Meaning of Immortality," *Improvement Era*, April 1955, 221.

Art Credits

iv–1. *For Unto Us* and detail of *For Unto Us* © 2009 Simon Dewey. Courtesy of Altus Fine Art. For print information go to www.altusfineart.com.

3. Detail of *Seeking the One* © 2009 Liz Lemon Swindle. Used with permission from Foundation Arts. For print information, go to www.foundationarts.com or call 1.800.366.2781.

4. *Prince of Peace* © 2009 Liz Lemon Swindle. Used with permission from Foundation Arts. For print information, go to www.foundationarts.com or call 1.800.366.2781.

6–7. *The Last Supper* and detail of *The Last Supper* © 2009 Simon Dewey. Courtesy of Altus Fine Art. For print information go to www.altusfineart.com.

9. *Broken Bread* © Walter Rane. For more information go to www.walterrane.com.

10–11. *Peace I Give Unto You* © Walter Rane. For more information go to www.walterrane.com.

12. *In Humility* © 2009 Simon Dewey. Courtesy of Altus Fine Art. For print information go to www.altusfineart.com.

15. *Washing Feet* © Jeffrey Hein. For more information, go to www.jeffreyhein.com.

16. *Bread and Wine* © 2009 Christopher Young. For print information, go to www.christopheryoungart.com.

18–19. *Last Supper* © Walter Rane. For more information go to www.walterrane.com.

20–21. Detail of *In Remembrance of Me* and *In Remembrance of Me* © Joseph F. Brickey. For more information, go to www.josephbrickey.com.

22. *Last Supper* © 2009 Liz Lemon Swindle. Used with permission from Foundation Arts. For print information, go to www.foundationarts.com or call 1.800.366.2781.

25. *Divine Redeemer* © 2009 Simon Dewey. Courtesy of Altus Fine Art. For print information go to www.altusfineart.com.

26–27. *Gethsemane* and detail of *Gethsemane* © 2009 Liz Lemon Swindle. Used with permission from Foundation Arts. For print information, go to www.foundationarts.com or call 1.800.366.2781.

29. *Oh My Father* © 2009 Simon Dewey. Courtesy of Altus Fine Art. For print information go to www.altusfineart.com.

30–31. *Gethsemane Grove* by Derek Hegsted © Derek Hegsted Fine Art. For print information, go to www.hegsted.com.

32. *Take Your Rest* © Walter Rane. For more information go to www.walterrane.com.

35. *Gethsemane* by James C. Christensen, © 2009 James C. Christensen, © The Greenwich Workshop ®, Inc. www.greenwichworkshop.com.

36. Atonement © Walter Rane. For more information go to www.walterrane.com.

38–39. *Gethsemane* © Adam Abram. For more information, visit www.olivewoodbooks.com.

41. *Son of the Highest* © Joseph F. Brickey. For more information, go to www.josephbrickey.com.

42–43. *Behold the Man* and detail of *Behold the Man* © 2009 Christopher Young. For print information, go to www.christopheryoungart.com.

45. *Peter's Denial* by Carl Heinrich Bloch. Courtesy of Det Nationalhistoriske Museum på Frederiksborg, Hillerød.

46. *The Lord Accused before Caiaphas* by Frank Adams.

48–49. *Behold the Man* © 2009 Simon Dewey. Courtesy of Altus Fine Art. For print information go to www.altusfineart.com.

51. *Jesus Scourged* by Gustave Doré, *The Doré Bible Illustrations*, Dover Publications.

52. *Christ with Crown of Thorns and Storm* etching by Carl Heinrich Bloch. Used courtesy of Hope Gallery. For print information, visit www.hopegallery.com.

55. *Man of Galilee* © Joseph F. Brickey. For more information, go to www.josephbrickey.com.

56–57. *Golgotha* and detail of *Golgotha* © 2009 Christopher Young. For print information, go to www.christopheryoungart.com.

59. *Jesus Falling Beneath the Cross* by Gustave Doré, *The Doré Bible Illustrations*, Dover Publications.

60–61. *Golgotha* by Derek Hegsted © Derek Hegsted Fine Art. For print information, go to www.hegsted.com.

62. *The Erection of the Cross* by Gustave Doré, *The Doré Bible Illustrations*, Dover Publications.

65. *Grey Day Golgotha* © J. Kirk Richards. For print information, go to www.jkirkrichards.com.

66. *Lamentation* © Joseph F. Brickey. For more information, go to www.josephbrickey.com.

68–69. *The Crucifixion* by Harry Anderson © Intellectual Reserve, Inc. Courtesy of the Church History Museum.

70–71. Detail of *It is Finished* and *It is Finished* © 2009 Liz Lemon Swindle. Used with permission from Foundation Arts. For print information, go to www.foundationarts.com or call 1.800.366.2781.

72. *Pieta* © Joseph F. Brickey. For more information, go to www.josephbrickey.com.

75. *Burial of Christ* by Carl Heinrich Bloch. Courtesy of Det Nationalhistoriske Museum på Frederiksborg, Hillerød.

76–77. *The Resurrection of Jesus Christ* and detail of *The Resurrection of Jesus Christ* © Patrick Devonas. From the collection of Michael Huffington. For print information, contact patrickdevonas@yahoo.com.

79. *Tomb* © Garth Oborn. For print information, send e-mail to annoborn@sisna.com or call 801.298.5694.

80–81. *Hope* © 2009 Liz Lemon Swindle. Used with permission from Foundation Arts. For print information, go to www.foundationarts.com or call 1.800.366.2781.

82 and back cover. *Risen Hope* © Joseph F. Brickey. For more information, go to www.josephbrickey.com.

84–85. *He is Not Here* © Walter Rane. For more information go to www.walterrane.com.

86. *Doubting Thomas* by Carl Heinrich Bloch. Used courtesy of Hope Gallery. For print information, visit www.hopegallery.com.

88–89. Detail of *The Living Christ* and *The Living Christ* © Joseph F. Brickey. For more information, go to www.josephbrickey.com.